Filipa Branco Azevedo

The Little
Making F

C000005503

by Keri Finlayson

Illustrations by Marion Lindsay

LITTLE BOOKS WITH **BIG** IDEAS

Published 2009 by A&C Black Publishers Limited
36 Soho Square, London W1D 3QY
www.acblack.com

ISBN 978-1-4081-1250-2

Text © Keri Finlayson
Illustrations © Marion Lindsay

A CIP record for this publication is available from the British Library.

Printed in Great Britain by Latimer Trend & Company Limited.

This book is produced using paper that is made from wood grown in
managed, sustainable forests. It is natural, renewable and recyclable.

The logging and manufacturing processes conform to the environmental
regulations of the country of origin.

**To see our full range of titles
visit www.acblack.com**

Contents

Introduction

Children love poetry. Those who care for the young know that children love to rhyme, to find rhythms and to play games with words. Young children develop language through vocal play, such as babies enjoying peek-a-boo games, toddlers repeating a favourite new word and pre-school children chanting nursery rhymes.

Young children find the language patterns in poetry fun, and will spontaneously create and play with rhyme, rhythm, assonance and alliteration for their own amusement. How many of us can still remember the rhymes we learned when we were very young? Remember the fascination of repeating sounds, the hilarity of attempting tongue twisters and the fun of skipping and clapping rhymes. The rhymes learned by children today are often very similar to those chanted by their parents and grandparents in nurseries and playgrounds long ago. Some rhymes such as 'Sing a song of sixpence' and 'Baa baa black sheep' have been recited by children for hundreds of years.

This desire to play with words and sounds, to create patterns and games, makes poetry an ideal vehicle not only for the learning of language and literacy skills, but also for learning about our natural, physical, social, personal and numerical world. Words spoken in rhythm and rhyme are words easily remembered, and poetry encourages children to learn and present new knowledge and skills in an entertaining, informative, creative and joyful way.

Making poetry and saying it out loud is fun. It allows children to develop confidence as individuals, encourages them to work together in a group and to feel a sense of belonging to the class as a whole. Saying rhymes aloud brings an unbeatable sense of triumph. It is an excellent way for young children to learn to speak clearly and with confidence. Those who can articulate clearly have enhanced phonic awareness, and this in turn reinforces emerging reading, writing and spelling skills. Children who have an understanding of rhyme and rhythm have an enriched understanding of language and feel confident and creative with literacy.

Using this book

The activities and suggestions in this book will help you and your children to create poetry together. Each activity is designed to increase phonic awareness as well as to encourage creativity and a love of words.

The activities are suitable for small groups of children as well as larger whole-class groups. Many of the activities can be carried out outdoors and involve equipment and materials that can be found in an everyday outdoor environment. Each activity is accompanied by a short list of the relevant Foundation Stage Development matters statements.

The activities and suggestions are designed for children in the Foundation Stage. The first three sections offer lots of ideas and activities to carry out with children at all stages of the Early Years Curriculum. The later sections of the book are created for older children, or for those who have developed the requisite phonological awareness. All the activities can be carried out as a whole or adapted according to your children's aptitudes and needs. Children have varying attention spans; you can shorten, lengthen or adapt the activities according to your professional judgement.

Language play often means letting the children take the lead, with the practitioner's role as that of an appreciative and encouraging audience! The poems and activities in this book enable practitioners to lay the foundations for poetry creation. The activities focus on inspiring creative language play and equipping children with the necessary skills to make their own poetry. Many of the activities are intended to develop descriptive language, to promote the enjoyment of rhyme and rhythm and to inspire creative writing, rather than act as guides to writing particular poems. Creating poetry is about enjoying the sound, the taste and the look of language. Encourage your children to be imaginative, to be creative and, most of all, to have fun with words!

The materials needed are listed at the beginning of each activity. Most items are to be found in any Early Years setting and, for many activities, the only things needed are enthusiastic voices and energetic bodies!

Chapter 1 shows you how to create a poetry-friendly environment. Children learn language and literacy in a social context – with the people and the world around them. In this chapter, you will find suggestions about how to make your setting one that inspires and fosters creative language play. It will also show you how to involve the wider community in your poetry making.

Chapters 2 and 3 look at the sounds that words make. These sections focus on the way a letter or group of letters sound (the phoneme). Chapter 2 looks at 'cvc' words and Chapter 3 looks at four common word endings.

Chapter 4 explores the jobs words do in a sentence. Here, children learn to make poems that encourage the creation of more complex sentences, moving from telegraphic to descriptive speech. These activities are suitable for older children or children who are confident with phonics, and can be adapted for younger children.

Chapter 5 gives a series of suggestions and templates for your own poetry creation, using techniques from the previous five sections. The poetry-making activities in this section are aimed at Reception children who can work more independently, but they can also be enjoyed by younger children.

Poetry creation and the EYFS

Poetry creation and language play involve the physical, emotional, social and intellectual development of the child. Making poetry is central to developing language and literacy skills. By exploring language and creating poetry, children can develop knowledge and skills in many areas: mathematical and scientific vocabulary is explored; motor skills are developed through mark-making; rhythm is explored with bodies through movement and dance; and social skills are enhanced as children create and recite rhymes together.

The Development matters statements in the Practice Guidance for the Early Years Foundation Stage contain many references to the skills that can be developed by poetry creation. The following statements are particularly relevant to poetry creation and language play.

Personal, Social and Emotional Development

Making poetry encourages children to express their thoughts, feelings and experiences, and to listen to those of others.

In Dispositions and Attitudes:

(40-60+m) ▶ Be confident to try new activities, initiate new ideas and speak in a familiar group (ELG).

▶ Maintain attention, concentrate, and sit quietly when appropriate, (ELG).

In Sense of Community:

(30-50m) ▶ Make connections between different parts of their life experience.

(40-60+m) ▶ Have an awareness of, and an interest in, cultural and religious differences.

Communication, Language and Literacy

In Language for Communication:

(30-50m) ▶ Use intonation, rhythm and phrasing to make their meaning clear to others.

▶ Join in with repeated refrains and anticipate key events and phrases in rhymes and stories.

(40-60+m) ▶ Listen with enjoyment and respond to stories and songs, and make up their own stories and poems (ELG).

▶ Extend their vocabulary, exploring the meanings and sounds of new words (ELG).

▶ Speak clearly and audibly with confidence and control, and show awareness of the listener (ELG).

In Linking Sounds and Letters:

(22-36m) ▶ Distinguish one sound from another.

▶ Show interest and play with sounds and rhymes.

(30-50m) ▶ Enjoy rhyming and rhymic activities.

▶ Show awareness of rhyme and alliteration.

▶ Recognise rhythm in spoken words.

(40-60+m) ▶ Continue a rhyming string.

In Reading:

(22-36m) ▶ Have some favourite stories, rhymes, songs, poems or jingles.

(30-50m) ▶ Listen to and join in with stories and poems, one-to-one and in small groups.

▶ Know information can be relayed in the form of print.

▶ Understand the concept of a word.

(40-60+m) ▶ Explore and experiment with sounds, words and texts (ELG).

In Writing:

(16-26m) ▶ Examine the marks they and others make.

(22-36m) ▶ Distinguish between different marks they make.

(30-50m) ▶ Use writing as a means of recording and communicating.

In Handwriting:

(30-50m) ▶ Use one-handed tools and equipment.

▶ Draw lines and circles using gross motor movements.

▶ Manipulate objects with increasing control.

(40-60+m) ▶ Begin to form recognisable letters.

Problem Solving, Reasoning and Numeracy

Numbers as Labels and for Counting:

(22-36m) ▶ Create and experiment with symbols and marks.

Shape, Space and Measures:

▶ Begin to categorise objects according to properties such as shape or size.

(30-50+m) ▶ Observe and use positional language.

Knowledge and Understanding of the World

Exploration and Investigation:

(30-50m) ▶ Show curiosity and interest in the features of objects and living things.

▶ Describe and talk about what they see.

In ICT:

(40-60+m) ▶ Use a mouse and keyboard to interact with age-appropriate computer software.

In Place:

(40-60+m) ▶ Notice differences between features of the local environment.

In Communities:

(22-36m) ▶ Are interested in others and their families.

(40-60+m) ▶ Gain an awareness of the cultures and beliefs of others.

Physical Development

In Movement and Space:

(22-36m) ▶ Respond to rhythm, music and story by means of gesture and movement.

▶ Manage body to create intended movements.

(30-50m) ▶ Use movement to express feelings.

In Using Equipment and Materials:

(22-36m) ▶ Show increasing control in holding and using hammers, books, beaters and mark-making tools.

(30-50m) ▶ Demonstrate increasing skill in the use of mark-making implements, blocks, construction and small-world activities.

(40-60+m) ▶ Explore malleable materials by patting, stroking, poking, squeezing, pinching and twisting them.

(40-60m) ▶ Use simple tools to effect changes to the materials

Creative Development

In Being Creative – Responding to Experiences, Expressing and Communicating Ideas:

(30-50m) ▶ Capture experiences and responses with music, dance, paint and other materials or words.

In Exploring Media and Materials:

(30-50m) ▶ Begin to be interested in and describe the texture of things.

▶ Differentiate marks and movements on paper.

In Creating Music and Dance:

(22-36m) ▶ Join in favourite songs.

▶ Create sounds by banging, shaking, tapping or blowing.

(30-50m) ▶ Sing a few familiar songs.

▶ Sing to themselves and make up simple songs.

▶ Tap out simple repeated rhythms and make some up.

Section

Creating the right environment

Early Years practitioners know how important it is to make their setting full of the sight and sound of language. By creating a word-rich environment where words are readily seen, heard and explored, children learn that words do many different jobs. They learn that words carry meaning, provide information and give pleasure. By creating a word-rich environment where word sounds are readily heard, children learn that spoken words can do many things. They learn that spoken words convey instructions, describe the physical world, and that their developing language enables them to describe and communicate their own thoughts, feelings, needs and wants. These developing language and emergent writing skills are fostered by enjoyment and play. Making poetry by exploring the sounds and patterns of language is an effective, creative and playful way of doing this.

By making your setting a word-rich environment, you are showing that language has an important purpose, and you are encouraging possibilities for language exploration and play.

The EYFS Practice Guidance states that the role of the practitioner is crucial in extending and developing children's language and communication in their setting.

In this section, you will find suggestions on how to extend and develop the language and communication of the children in your care, and to help make your setting come alive with the written and spoken word through poetry and language play.

Remember to:

▶ display written words and texts with the child's eye line in mind. Try sitting on the floor in various parts of your setting and seeing the environment as a child does.

▶ create displays that have a good mixture of clear text and bright, colourful pictures.

▶ create a reading area or book corner that has plenty of poetry books and rhyming stories. Try featuring a range of different books each week in your reading area. You could feature a story book, a poetry book and a non-fiction book.

▶ create labels for objects in your setting, such as 'cupboard', 'wall', 'door' and 'window', and for specific areas, such as 'water area', 'sand area' or 'shop'.

▶ add examples of instructional writing, such as 'three people in the sand area', four people in the house or 'please wash your hands'.

Make an inspiration table

Descriptive language is an important part of making poetry. You can help children to develop their vocabulary and encourage them to think of new ways to communicate their ideas about their world, by providing springboards of inspiration. Creating an inspiration table is a good way to do this.

What you need

- a display table
- leaves and twigs
- a vase of flowers
- pebbles and stones
- shells
- interesting fabric

Preparation

Collect interesting objects for your table. These can be man-made or natural objects. Choose a variety of things that have lots of different properties: things that are smooth, rough, hard, soft, heavy or light. Look for things that can be handled safely, making sure that the objects you have choosen have no sharp edges or bits that can be easily broken off or put in the mouth. Place the objects on your display table.

Key words	
rough	heavy
smooth	light
hard	
soft	

EYFS Development matters statements

CLL (40-60+m) Extend their vocabulary, exploring the meanings and sounds of new words.

PSRN (22-36m) Begin to categorise objects according to properties such as shape or size.

KUW (30-50m) Show curiosity and interest in the features of objects and living things.

KUW (30-50m) Describe and talk about what they see.

What you do

▶ Gather a small group of children in a circle on the carpet and place a selection of your objects in the middle, making sure everyone can see.

▶ Explain that some objects have to be handled gently or they may break or tear.

▶ Ask which of the objects might tear or break if you pull them.

▶ Pass the objects to the children and encourage them to touch, handle and even smell them.

▶ When you say 'pass it on please', each child must pass their object to the person next to them.

▶ When everyone in the group has handled all the objects, place them back to the middle of the circle.

▶ Talk about each object in turn and explore words you could use to describe it. What colour is it? What does it feel like? Is it rough or smooth? Is it heavy or light? Is it hard or soft?

▶ Focus on the words the children use to describe the object and on any new words that you introduce. Repeat the words clearly. As you repeat the word, ask the children to say it with you, emphasising the sound of the word.

▶ Can you see other things around you that can be described in the same way? For example: The stone is smooth, so smooth. What else is smooth? This cup is smooth. This brick is smooth.

▶ Change the objects on display regularly to maintain interest and extend new vocabulary.

▶ Repeat the carpet activity with new objects, reinforcing describing words and exploring new ones, such as 'bumpy', 'wrinkly', 'shiny' and 'slippery'.

Further fun

▶ Encourage parents and carers to bring in interesting objects that might act as a springboard for descriptive language.

▶ Ask the children to bring in objects from a holiday or visit. Make sure they have permission from their parents or carers and that the carer understands that the object is to be handled by the children.

▶ Look in charity shops and car boot sales for unusual objects with interesting properties that could capture young imaginations.

Make an inspiration board

Talking about images stimulates descriptive language as children find ways to communicate what they see. Make an inspiration board that will stimulate descriptive language, by displaying photographs and pictures from magazines and newspapers.

What you need

- sugar paper or cork board
- drawing pins
- sticky-tack
- photographs
- magazines (home decoration and gardening magazines are particularly good)
- leaflets
- scissors

Preparation

Collect sources of interesting images. Look for scenes and images that are clear and identifiable: home decorating, travel magazines and catalogues are particularly useful as they will contain images of familiar objects. Cover an area of wall with sugar paper or cork board. Remember to keep it at child eye level so they can get up close and have a good look!

Key words	
tall	red
short	yellow
big	blue
small	green

EYFS Development matters statements

CLL (30-50m) Begin to use more complex sentences.

CLL (40-60+m) Extend their vocabulary, exploring the meanings and sounds of new words.

KUW (30-50m) Show curiosity and interest in the features of objects and living things.

KUW (30-50m) Describe and talk about what they see.

What you do

▶ Offer a range of magazines to a group of children. Make sure there are enough for one each if needed.

▶ Encourage the children to look at the pictures in the magazines and to find pictures that interest them.

▶ Discuss what or who is in the pictures they find.

▶ Ask what is happening in the pictures.

▶ Focus on words you could use to describe the objects or people in the pictures. Are they big or small, tall or short?

▶ Discuss the colours you can see.

▶ Reinforce new descriptive vocabulary by repeating it and emphasising the sound of the word.

▶ Let the children cut out pictures that particularly appeal to them. (Many children will need assistance with scissor skills; encourage independence without allowing frustration to overtake!)

Ask each child to place their favourite picture on the inspiration board and encourage them to describe what they see. Repeat their statements to the other children, emphasising their use of descriptive words. For example, 'Jon has found a picture of a big, red teapot.' 'Sami has found a picture of a tall mountain. He says it looks cold.'

Further fun

▶ Encourage children to bring in pictures of their own. If they bring in family photographs, make sure you have permission from the parent or carer to display them.

Sound letter boxes

Recognising initial letter sounds is one of the first steps in gaining phonic awareness. Make letter boxes and encourage role play with letter sounds.

What you need

▶ shoeboxes with lids

▶ red poster paint

▶ glue sticks

▶ drawing materials

▶ paper

▶ magazines

▶ scissors

▶ a computer with printer

▶ thick marker pens

Preparation

First, paint your shoebox red. When it is dry, cut a large oblong opening in the lid suitable for posting letters. Now you have a letter box! Next, decide on the initial letter that you are going to focus on and find a selection of pictures of things that start with that letter. Look in magazines, print them from the internet, or draw some yourself if you are confident! Introduce the children to your chosen initial letter sound, or reinforce previous initial letter activities by discussing familiar words that begin with your chosen letter and discussing your pictures.

EYFS Development matters statements

CLL (22-36m) Distinguish one sound from another.

CLL (30-50m) Hear and say the initial sound in words and know which letters represent some of the sounds.

CLL (30-50m) Show awareness of rhyme and alliteration.

CLL (30-50m) Explore and experiment with sounds, words and texts.

What you do

▶ Choose your initial letter, 'a' for example, and compile your 'a' pictures.

▶ Seat the children on the carpet with you, your 'a' pictures, the shoebox and a glue stick.

▶ Discuss with the children things that start with the 'a' sound. Include people's names.

▶ Show the children the box and say it is an 'a' letter box.

▶ Take a picture of an 'a' object and glue it on the a box.

▶ Write the appropriate initial letter above the slot on the lid with a thick black marker pen, showing the children as you do so.

▶ Ask the children to help you to post the pictures in the box.

▶ Now seat the children at tables and provide them with crayons or coloured pencils and paper.

▶ Ask the children to draw some things that start with the 'a' sound. This could be an apple, an ant or a friend called Anna.

▶ Place the letter box on an accessible table and as the children finish their pictures, they can post them in the box.

▶ Create more boxes for more letter sounds.

Further fun

▶ Collect old envelopes and encourage the children to fold their pictures and place them inside before posting.

▶ 'Address' the envelope and stamp with a fun stamp.

▶ Make a posting area by stacking sound letter boxes against a wall and providing paper and writing materials for letters.

▶ Provide postmens' caps and delivery bags for role play.

▶ Encourage older children to make attempts at writing and posting words.

Rhyme boxes

Recognising the middle vowel sound in cvc words will help with reading and spelling later on. Make rhyme boxes and pretend to be rhyming post people!

What you need

▶ shoeboxes with lids

▶ red poster paint

▶ glue sticks

▶ drawing materials

▶ paper

▶ magazines

▶ scissors

▶ computer with printer

Preparation

Paint your shoebox red. When it is dry, cut a large rectangular opening in the lid suitable for posting letters.

Decide on the middle vowel sound that you are going to focus on for this letter box and choose one simple image for that sound that is commonly found and easy to draw.

For example: a – cat   e – pen   i – bin   o – dog   u – sun.

Introduce the children to your chosen sound or reinforce previous middle rhyme activities by discussing familiar words that rhyme with your chosen word.

EYFS Development matters statements

CLL (22-36m) Distinguish one sound from another

CLL (22-36m) Show interest and play with sounds and rhymes.

CLL (30-50m) Enjoy rhyming and rhyming activities.

CLL (30-50m) Show awareness of rhyme and alliteration.

CLL (40-60+m) Explore and experiment with sounds, words and texts.

What you do

▶ Choose your rhyme sound and compile your pictures. If you are focusing on the 'a' sound and the word 'cat', for example, collect as many pictures of cats as you can.

▶ Seat the children on the carpet with you, your cat pictures, the box and a glue stick each.

▶ Discuss with the children things that have an 'a' sound in the middle, as in cat. Include people's names.

▶ Show the children the box and tell them that it is a rhyme box for words that all have an 'a' sound in them, like the word cat.

▶ Take one of your cat pictures and glue it on to the box.

▶ Using a thick black marker pen, write the whole word (for example, cat) above the slot on the lid, showing the children as you do so.

▶ Place the lid on your rhyme box, hold up one of your pictures and post it in.

▶ Now seat the children at tables and provide them with crayons or coloured pencils and paper.

▶ Ask the children to draw cats or things that rhyme with cat.

▶ When the children have finished their pictures, they can post them in the rhyme box.

Further fun

▶ Collect old envelopes and encourage the children to fold their pictures and place them inside before posting.

▶ 'Address' the envelope and stamp with a fun stamp.

▶ Make a posting area by stacking rhyme boxes against a wall and providing paper and drawing materials for pictures.

▶ Provide postmens' caps and delivery bags for role play.

▶ Encourage older children to make attempts at writing and posting their own words.

Make your own poetry book

By creating their own magical poetry book, children can see the rhymes they know reproduced in print and contained in a very special place.

What you need

- a selection of poetry books with illustrations
- a notebook
- a large scrapbook
- glue
- writing materials
- plain paper
- shiny materials for decorating (sequins, ribbons, glitter, foil shapes etc.)
- a computer with printer

Preparation

Spend time discussing rhymes that the children know or enjoy saying. These can be nursery rhymes or lullabies they know from home, or rhymes you sing together in your setting. Show them a selection of poetry books and look at the text and the illustrations. Discuss the fact that the illustrations are about things that are happening in the text. Tell the children that they are going to make their own very special poetry book.

EYFS Development matters statements

CLL (22-36m) Have available some favourite stories, rhymes, songs, poems and jingles.

CLL (30-50m) Listen and join in with stories and poems, one-to-one and in small groups.

CLL (30-50m) Know information can be relayed in the form of print.

CLL (30-50m) Show interest in illustrations and print in books, and print in the environment.

CLL (30-50m) Handle books carefully.

CLL (30-50m) Hold books the correct way up and turn pages.

What you do

▶ Ask children individually or in small groups for rhymes they know or like.

▶ Write these in a notebook as the children recite them with or without your help, making sure that they see you do this and are aware of what you are doing.

▶ Show them the rhyme in your notebook when you have written it.

▶ Print out each rhyme on the computer in a large clear font with the title at the top and the names of the child or children who suggested it to you at the bottom.

▶ Show the children the printed poems and their names.

▶ Stick each of the poems into a large scrapbook.

▶ Print out or write the words 'Our Poetry Book' in large letters on the front cover.

▶ Decorate the front and back cover with shiny and glittery materials to give a sparkly, jewelled effect. Ask the children to help you!

Display your book where everyone can admire it!

Further fun

▶ Make mini books by folding and stapling scrap paper together for children to write in and illustrate.

Recording your poetry

Record your poetry recitation for everyone to hear and enjoy.

What you need

▶ recording equipment such as a tape recorder, a computer with a microphone or alternative sound-recording device

Preparation

Read and recite lots of rhymes, poems and songs as a group. More confident children may have a favourite rhyme or song they are keen to say out loud, by themselves or with a friend. Send a letter home to parents and carers telling them that you are going to make a poetry recording. Ask if there are any volunteers who would like to come in to recite and record a rhyme or poem they can remember from when they were a child.

EYFS Development matters statements

PSED (40-60m) Be confident to try new activities, initiate new ideas and speak in a familiar group.

CLL (30-50m) Use intonation, rhythm and phrasing to make their meaning clear to others.

KUW (40-60+m) Use a mouse or a keyboard to interact with age-appropriate computer software.

CD (30-50m) Sing a few familiar songs.

CD (22-36m) Join in favourite songs.

What you do

▶ Hold a poetry recording week.

▶ Set some time aside each day to practise and record one or two poems.

▶ Say the title of the poem and who is reciting it before each poem.

▶ Include examples of short poems, nursery rhymes, chants and games.

▶ Arrange for parents and carers to visit and record a reading of a poem that they have enjoyed.

▶ Make the recording freely available in your setting for children (and others) to listen to.

Sit and listen to the recording you've made or play it in the backgound as other activities take place.

Further fun

Make further recordings for different themes, such as:

▶ weather rhymes

▶ animal rhymes

▶ rhymes from festivals.

Make links with your local community

Poetry and song is something that people of all ages, and from all communities, enjoy. Young and old alike can benefit from sharing rhymes and enjoying each other's company.

See if you can visit a local home for the elderly, or a day or community centre, and record or listen to residents reciting favourite rhymes and playground chants from their childhood. Prepare your visit well in advance by writing or visiting in person. Explain that you are collecting rhymes and poems from the past. Ask if people remember any rhymes from their childhood and if they would like to have these written down or recorded for the children in your setting. You could either arrange to visit with the children or make time to visit yourself and record their rhymes. Remember to write a thank you letter from you and the children.

▶ Invite a small group of local residents from a church or community to a performance of nursery rhymes at your setting, if you have room. Keep the performance short and always perform with the childen yourself. (If shyness takes over, yours may be the only voice!) Provide refreshments: biscuits and juice go down well with performance poets and audiences of all ages!

▶ Try to collect rhymes in different languages. Ask the children in your setting if they can say any rhymes in a language other than English. Ask parents and carers who speak a language other than English if they could visit and recite a rhyme. Can the children all learn a rhyme or a clapping game in another language? Can they find out what it is about?

EYFS Development matters statements ————————————————

PSED (30-50m) Show increasing confidence in new situations.

Talk freely about their home and community.

PSED (30-50m) Form good relationships with adults and peers.

PSED (40-60+m) Have an awareness of, and an interest in, cultural and religious differences.

CLL (40-60+m) Listen with enjoyment and respond to stories, songs and other music, rhymes and poems.

CLL (40-60+m) Speak clearly and audibly with confidence and control.

Create a rhythm-rich environment

Hearing the rhythm in words and sentences is an important step in gaining phonic awareness. Make your setting a rhythm-rich environment by providing lots of opportunities to stamp out a rhythm and make some noise!

Clap the beat!

Clapping along to a poem or song is an excellent way of feeling and understanding rhythm. Clapping helps children to become aware of the fact that words have different numbers of syllables. Syllables are the beats you can hear in a word.

For example:

Cat has one syllable or beat.

Kitten (kit-ten) has two syllables or beats.

What you do

▶ Can the children all clap in time together? Try clapping a number of beats to see if the children can clap the same number back.

▶ Clap fast beats and slow beats, loud beats and soft beats.

▶ Clap your names. Take it in turns to say your full names, with everyone repeating it and clapping the number of beats (syllables).

For example:

Ke-ri, Lou-ise, Fin-lay-son = seven claps

Jack-Hall = two claps.

▶ Clap along to your favourite rhymes as you say them.

Try clapping along to:

Pat-a-cake, pat-a-cake, baker's man.
Bake me a cake as fast as you can.
Pat it and roll it and mark it with B
And put it in the oven for baby and me.

Be your own rhythm instrument

You can clap with your hands to make a rhythm and you can also use the rest of your body too! It is important that young children use their whole bodies when learning. Research has shown that early learning is active learning. By responding to language with arms and legs, hands and feet, children develop important motor skills that enable further learning.

Be your own rhythm instrument by slapping your hands on your knees. Can the children slap their hands on their knees and then clap their hands together?

What you do

Can they slap their right hand on their left knee and their left hand on their right knee? (This is very tricky!)

▶ Create some slap patterns on your knees for these rhymes:

I like coffee I like tea.
I like friends to play with me.
Flee fly flee.
Don't sit on my knee.
Shoo fly shoo.
Don't sit on my shoe.

EYFS Development matters statements

CD (30-50m) Capture experiences and responses with music, dance, paint and other materials or words.

CLL (30-50m) Recognise rhythm in spoken words.

PD (22-36m) Respond to rhythm, music and story by means of gesture and movement.

PD (22-36m) Combine and repeat a range of movements.

CD (30-50m) Tap out simple repeated rhythms and make some up.

CD (40-60+m) Begin to move rhythmically.

Make your own percussion instuments

Use junk materials to create a rhythm orchestra!

Make rhythm shakers

What you need

- empty plastic bottles with lids
- beads
- dried beans or pasta
- plastic funnels

What you do

- Half fill plastic bottles (use large and small empty bottles) with beans, dried lentils or plastic or wooden beads.
- Children can help to fill their bottle with beads or beans using a funnel.
- Make sure the lid to the container is screwed back on very tightly.
- Shake to the rhythm!

Make a rain stick

What you need

- cardboard tubes
- thick paper
- tape
- beads, dried beans or pasta
- plastic funnels

What you do

► Seal the end of a long cardboard tube with thick paper and tape.

► Fill with dried lentils, pasta or beads. Children can pour the beads or pasta in using a funnel.

► Seal the other end.

► Decorate your rain stick.

► Tip from end to end to make a long, slow beat or shake quickly.

Bang your own drum

Drums can be made out of almost anything. Try making drums out of:

► empty boxes of all shapes and sizes – shoeboxes, packing boxes, cereal boxes etc.

► plastic tubs and bowls

► upturned empty bins.

Use percussion instruments

Create a music box for the setting and fill it with instruments that you have made as well as the following traditional percussion instruments:

► triangles
► maracas
► tambourines
► bells
► castanets
► mini xylophones.

EYFS Development matters statements

CD (22-36m) Create sounds by banging, shaking, tapping or blowing.

CD (30-50m) Explore and learn how sounds can be changed.

CD (40-60+m) Explore the different sounds of instruments.

Create a word-sound-rich environment

The EYFS states that practitioners should successfully create settings that enable learning and development.

It states that practitioners should attempt to:

▶ give daily opportunities to share and enjoy a wide range of fiction and non-fiction books, rhymes, music, songs, poetry and stories.

▶ provide an environment that is rich in signs, symbols, notices, numbers, words, rhymes, books, pictures, music and songs that take into account children's different interests, understandings, home backgrounds and cultures.

▶ link language with physical movement in action songs and rhymes, role play and practical experiences, such as cookery and gardening.

▶ talk to children and engage them as partners in conversation.

Be word aware

As a practitioner, you know that your use of language has a huge influence on the language development of the children in your setting.

▶ Always make sure you are facing the child and are making eye contact when having a conversation. Bend down or sit on the floor to bring yourself to eye level.

▶ Make your speech clear and your face expressive and interested.

▶ Ask questions! By having a conversation with a child, you are promoting language skills and teaching new vocabulary as well as enhancing self-esteem. It's always nice when someone is interested in what you are saying, whether you are three or thirty-three!

▶ Make sure you spend time listening to each child speak. This can be difficult in the hustle and bustle of an Early Years setting, but it is extremely beneficial, even if you focus on a one-to-one exchange with a child for just a few moments.

▶ Repeat a phrase or a word back to the child if they have trouble pronouncing it.

For example:

Child: 'I have a new dod!'
Teacher: 'How exciting! You have a new **dog**! What's its name?'

Read poetry

The way you read poetry and your attitude to it will influence the way your children enjoy poetry.

▶ Show your enthusiasm for language by acting the poem and exaggerating your facial expressions.

▶ Make sure that when you read a poem you make clear distinctions between the words.

▶ It usually helps to read a poem to yourself before you read it to the children. That way, you can feel the rhythm of the poem and are able to communicate it fully when you say the poem out loud.

Learning to recite poetry

The ability to learn things 'by heart' is a very valuable skill and one that can be improved with practice, even at a very early age. Reciting poetry to an audience of friends, parents or carers gives confidence. Recitation should always be fun and never a chore. Young children spontaneously memorise rhymes and songs that they use in play. As a practitioner, you can introduce rhymes and songs that they can incorporate into their play world such as **Miss Polly had a dolly** for hospital role play, or **Polly put the kettle on** for play in the house.

Ways with words and word games

You can make your setting into a word-sound-rich environment by inviting others to come into your setting to read or recite poetry to the children. Keep the readings short and make sure your visitors understand that your children are young and have varying concentration spans.

You could:

▶ Invite a local poet to your setting to give a reading or run a workshop. Your local library should have information about poets in your area.

▶ Ask parents or grandparents to visit and recite rhymes they learned as children. This could be for part of a session or parents and carers could pop in just before collection time to say a rhyme for the children.

▶ Organise for children from a local primary school to visit and read poems that they have written. Making links is usually always beneficial for all concerned.

Clapping and skipping games

Clapping and skipping games are an excellent way of getting to grips with rhyme and ryhthm. Play clapping games inside and outside your setting, such as:

A sailor went to sea

A sailor went to sea sea sea,
To see what he could see see see,
But all that he could see see see,
Was the bottom of the deep blue sea sea sea.

Or play skipping games, such as:

Teddy bear, teddy bear

Teddy Bear, Teddy Bear, touch the ground,
Teddy Bear, Teddy Bear, show your shoe,
Teddy Bear, Teddy Bear, turn around,
Teddy Bear, Teddy Bear, touch the ground,
Teddy Bear, Teddy Bear, show your shoe,
Teddy Bear, Teddy Bear, that will do!
Teddy Bear, Teddy Bear, climb the stairs,
Teddy Bear, Teddy Bear, say your prayers,
Teddy Bear, Teddy Bear, turn out the light,
Teddy Bear, Teddy Bear, say goodnight.

Play with tongue twisters

Tongue twisters are an excellent way to practise speaking clearly and are always enormous fun.

Try saying:

- A box of biscuits.
- Red lorry, yellow lorry.
- Toy boat, toy boat.
- Sam's shop sells spotty socks.
- Crisp crusts crackle.

Make some tongue twisters of your own

Think of three words that begin with the same letter and try saying them quickly, one after another. Can you find three things that start with the same sound in your setting?

For instance:

- brick bat ball
- red rabbit run
- custard cat can
- sun sea sand.

Make a weekly challenge tongue-twister board

▶ Place a large piece of sugar paper or card on the wall near the entrance to your setting.

▶ Write or print out a tongue twister in large letters and pin it on to your board.

▶ Put a new tongue twister up every week and challenge people (including visiting adults) to say it.

Rhyme time and story time

Make poetry reading an everyday activity in your setting. As a practitioner, you can show your love of poetry by talking about the poems and rhymes you enjoy and making rhyme time part of story time.

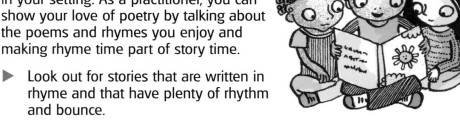

▶ Look out for stories that are written in rhyme and that have plenty of rhythm and bounce.

▶ You could start story time with a few tongue twisters to warm up, recite some rhymes, then read a new poem and discuss it. Now, when you start your story, the children's ears are alive to the sounds and rhythms of language, whether the story you have chosen for the day is rhyming or not.

EYFS Development matters statements ――――――――――――――

PSED (40-60+m) Be confident to try new activities, initiate new ideas and speak in a familiar group.

PSED (40-60+m) Maintain attention, concentrate and sit quietly when appropriate.

CLL (30-50m) Use intonation, rhythm and phrasing to make their meaning clear to others.

CLL (30-50m) Join in with repeated refrains and anticipate key events and phrases in rhymes and stories.

CLL (40-60+m) Listen with enjoyment and respond to stories and songs, and make up their own stories and poems.

CLL (40-60+m) Extend their vocabulary, exploring the meanings and sounds of new words.

CLL (40-60+m) Speak clearly and audibly with confidence and control, and show awareness of the listener.

Using computers

Poetry websites

There are many good poetry websites for children and they can be an invaluable resourse for the Early Years practitioner (see page 80).

► Poetry websites are a good place to find new poems, poems about a particular theme or information about a poet.

► Many poets have their own websites where you can find biographical information, interesting facts about their work and whether they can be booked for author visits.

► You can use search engines, such as Google, to search for types of poem.

► You could search for poems about particular topics, for example, weather or animal poems. If you know the title and author, you can search for particular poems.

Using the printer

Printers can be used to produce work in quantity that is clear, creative and colourful. Use your printer to:

► Print out the children's poetry creations. Display them around your setting or in a scrapbook.

► Print out famous poems and popular rhymes, and display them in your setting or in your own 'collection'.

► Make your own labels for objects around your setting. Laminate labels for objects in your outdoor area, if you have one.

► Make flash cards. Use them for the activities in this book or to play flash card games, such as 'Rhyme snap'.

Rhyme snap

▶ This game can be played by older children who are developing letter recognition, but it can also be played by younger children who can recognise the shape of the coloured letter in the middle of each word.

▶ Print and make flash cards of cvc words (consonant-vowel-consonant words) such as cat or big.

▶ Highlight the middle vowel by making it bold or by making it a different colour.

▶ Play snap, making the vowel sound as you lay the card down.

If both the players say the same sound, the first to say 'snap!' wins the pile.

Using the tool bar

Highlighting and changing the appearance and size of letters and words on the computer screen is a fun way for young children to become familiar with letter shapes and gain letter recognition.

You could:

▶ Experiment with different fonts. Show the children how to change the appearance of a piece of writing by changing the font. Do different fonts make the writing look serious, funny, silly or pretty?

▶ List cvc words with the same middle vowel sound and make that vowel sound bold or a different size or font.

Make a letter cloud picture poem

▶ Write letters all over the screen in different sizes and fonts as many times as you can. Print and cut out the letters. Stick the words onto a piece of coloured paper to create a beautiful cloud effect.

EYFS Development matters statements

KUW/ICT (40-60+m) Use a mouse and keyboard to interact with age appropriate computer software.

Section

Making rhymes (with cvc words)

The first rhymes that young children encounter and learn to reproduce themselves are often 'cvc' rhymes. When developing literacy skills, these are also the first words children learn to read and spell. The ability to hear the short vowel sound in the middle of these words, and then to match it to other words that have the same sound, is an important step in developing language and literacy skills.

What are cvc words?

'cvc' stands for consonant-vowel-consonant. Vowels are the letters **a**, **e**, **i**, **o** and **u**. Consonants are all the other letters in the alphabet. A cvc word is a three-letter word that has a vowel in the middle and a consonant on either side, such as **dog**, **cat** or **sun**. The vowel sounds here are **short**: **a** as in **cat**, not long as in **cake**; **i** as in **pin**, not long as in pine.

The poems in this chapter focus on cvc rhymes. They encourage children to recognise the middle vowel sound and match it to others. Each of these poems and accompanying activities encourages the recognition of the five vowels as both sounds and written letters. At the start of each poem, the short vowel sound is repeated eight times. It's important that the sound is correctly pronounced at the beginning of the activity so that it can be heard in other words, and so that the correct letter shape is matched to the correct sound later on.

Some cvc words

a

bag man

can hat

rat pan

i

pin pig

wig big

bin hit

e

pen pet

den ten

get yes

o

pot mop

hot dog

dot top

u

fun sun

rug nut

bun pup

Sandy Rabbit

This poem enables children to:

▶ recognise the 'a' sound;
▶ recognise the letter a.

a a a a
a a a a
**Ab Dab Sandy Rabbit
wanted the bat but
couldn't have it.
Ab Dab Sandy Rabbit
ran around and tried to
grab it.**

What you need

▶ sticky-tack
▶ fur fabric, felt or card circles (2cm) to make rabbit tails

What you do

▶ Read through the poem, emphasising the short 'a' sound in each word and pointing to each word as you say it.

▶ Ask the children to open their mouths wide and say the short 'a' sound as quickly and sharply as they can.

▶ Now ask the children to say the rhyme with you, stressing the sharp, quick 'a' sound.

- ▶ Cut 20 small circles of fur fabric, felt or card to make the rabbit tails.

- ▶ Put a blob of sticky-tack on the back of each one.

- ▶ Write the poem on a whiteboard, leaving a gap between each line, or write or print it out and pin it up.

- ▶ Read out the poem again, emphasising the short 'a' sound and pointing to the **a**.

- ▶ Put the rabbit tails into a container. Pick one out and stick it above the first letter **a**.

- ▶ Ask for volunteers to pick out a tail and stick it above the next letter 'a', saying a short, sharp **a** as they do so.

Further fun

- ▶ Replace the word bat with another cvc word.
- ▶ Read your new poem together.

EYFS Development matters statements

PSED (40-60+m) Maintain attention, concentrate and sit quietly when appropriate.

CLL (22-36m) Distinguish one sound from another.

CLL (40-60+m) Continue a rhyming string.

Best pen pet

This poem enables children to:

▶ recognise the short 'e' sound; recognise the letter **e**;

▶ complete a poem using the short 'e' sound

e e e e
e e e e
With my pen I can make a pet.
It will be my best pet yet.
What shall I call my best pen pet?
I will call him ... Ben.

What you need

▶ voices

What you do

Making the short 'e' sound:

▶ Practise saying the 'e' sound. Make the sound short and sharp.

▶ Read the poem, emphasising the short 'e' sounds.

Making a short **e** poem:

▶ Read out and discuss the cvc **e** words.

▶ Can you think of more words that have the short 'e' sound?

▶ Can you think of some silly words?

▶ Now think up some names for the pet in the poem. It can be any word that has the short 'e' sound and it can be as silly as you like.

Read the poem, replacing Ben with your own name suggestions.

Further fun

Make pen pets:

▶ Give each child a picture of a large lower case **e** that has been drawn or printed on a piece of A4 paper.

▶ Turn the **e** into a pet by adding a tail, ears, eyes and whiskers by drawing them on with pens or crayons.

EYFS Development matters statements ——————

CLL (22-36m) Distinguish one sound from another.
CLL (40-60+m) Continue a rhyming string.

Iggy Pig

i i i i

i i i i

Iggy Pig.
Iggy Pig.
Where is Iggy Pig?
Is he hiding in the bin?
What is in the bin with him?
Does it have an i in it?

This poem enables children to:

▶ recognise the short 'i' sound;

▶ pronounce the short 'i' sound;

▶ create short 'i' rhymes.

What you need

▶ a toy pig or a picture of a pig

▶ a bin or other similar container

▶ several familiar objects or pictures of objects that can be placed in the container that don't have the short 'i' sound

▶ several objects that have the short 'i' sound in their name, such as a safety pin, a tin of beans, a wig and a stick. (If you don't have these, find or make pictures of them instead.)

What you do

▶ Practice making the short 'i' sound. Open your mouth, smile and say a short sharp 'i'.

▶ Read the poem Iggy Pig.

- ▶ Try saying the words Iggy Pig several times. Shout it out loud if you want to.
- ▶ Place all the items in your bin in front of the children, naming them as they go in.
- ▶ Say the poem with the children joining in. Ask for a volunteer to close their eyes and pick out an item.
- ▶ Say the last two lines of the poem as they hold up the object and see if the item picked does have an **i** in it.

Further fun

- ▶ Go for a walk and see how many things you can see that contain the short 'i' sound e.g., hill, window-sill and shop till.
- ▶ See if anybody's name has the short 'i' sound.

EYFS Development matters statements

CLL (22-36m) Distinguish one sound from another.

CLL (22-36m) Show interest and play with sounds and rhymes.

CLL (30-50m) Enjoy rhyming and rhyming activities.

CLL (30-50m) Show awareness of rhyme and alliteration.

KUW (30-50m) Show curiosity and interest in the features of objects and living things.

What dog? Hot dog!

o o o o
o o o o

What dog?	What dog?
Hot dog!	Mop dog!
What dog?	Hot, spot, log, mop.
Spot dog!	What a lot of dogs we've got!
What dog?	
Log dog!	

This poem enables children to:

▶ recognise the short 'o' sound;

▶ say the short 'o' sound;

▶ create rhymes with the short 'o' sound.

What you need

▶ your voices!

▶ a toy dog or a picture of a dog

▶ the poem 'What dog? Hot dog!' either written on a board or pinned up on a sheet.

What you do

▶ Make your mouth into a tight round shape and say short, sharp o's.

▶ Draw **o** shapes in the air with your finger as you make the sound, starting at the top of the 'o' and returning to the top.

▶ Can you think of any other word that has the short 'o' sound?

▶ Read through the poem, emphasising the short 'o' sound as you say it. Make your own dog rhyme by asking 'What dog?' and getting the children to think of an 'o' word response. For example, top, pot, mop, dot, not, lot, cot and pop.

Further fun

Make a spot dog

▶ Print an outline of a dog.

▶ Fill it with 'os' drawn with felt pens or crayons.

Play 'I spot a spot'

Place dot stickers around your setting and ask the children to hunt for the spots. When they find one, they should shout 'o o o! I spot a spot!'

EYFS Development matters statements

CLL (30-50m) Draw lines and circles using gross motor movements.

CLL (40-60m) Begin to form recognisable letters.

CLL (22-36m) Distinguish one sound from another.

CLL (22-36m) Show interest and play with sounds and rhymes.

CLL (30-50m) Enjoy rhyming and rhyming activities.

CLL (30-50m) Show awareness of rhyme and alliteration.

Up! Up! Up!

u u u u
u u u u

Up! Up! Up!.
I can reach the bun bun.
Up! Up! Up!.
I can reach my tum tum.
Up! Up! Up!.
I can reach the sun sun.
Up! Up! Up!.
I'm having lots of fun fun.

This poem enables children to:

▶ recognise the short 'u' sound;

▶ say the short 'u' sound;

▶ create rhymes with the short 'u' sound.

What you need

▶ your voices
▶ your fingers

What you do

▶ Open your mouth and drop your chin down, making short, sharp 'u' sounds from the middle of your chest.

▶ Write the letter 'u' in the air with your fingers as you say the sound.

▶ Read the poem, emphasising the 'u' sound and pointing to the words as you say them.

▶ Think of other cvc **u** words. Say them out loud, emphasising the **u**.

▶ Read the poem again, choosing new **u** words and making up an action for them. You could stroke the **pup**, shake the **rug**, eat the **nut**, splash in the **mud** and tickle the **cub**.

EYFS Development matters statements

CLL (40-60+m) Begin to form recognisable letters.

CLL (22-36m) Distinguish one sound from another.

CLL (22-36m) Show interest and play with sounds and rhymes.

CLL (30-50m) Enjoy rhyming and rhyming activities.

CLL (30-50m) Show awareness of rhyme and alliteration.

Section

Making rhymes (endings)

In this section, there are poems and activities about four common word endings:

▶ ing

▶ ang

▶ and

▶ end.

The mouth makes several sounds with these endings. It is important to sound out the ending clearly and all the way to the last letter, for example, e-n-d – i-ng.

This will help with spelling later on and promote clear speech now.

Spend some time exploring the sounds in these endings. Start by focusing on the initial vowel sound and make sure this is clear and distinct. Then add the **ng** or **nd**, stressing the **g** or **d** sound at the end but not prolonging it.

At the start of each poem, the word ending is repeated four times. It's important that the focus sound is correctly pronounced at the beginning of the activity so that it can be spotted in other words, and so that the correct letters can be matched to the correct sound.

Things go ding! (a noisy poem)

ing ing ing ing
ing ing ing ing

A thing can ding.
A thing can ping.
A thing can swing or sing or sting.
But we love things that ding!
A bell can ding. DING. DING. DING.
A triangle can ding. DING. DING. DING.
DING! DING! DING!
We love things that ding!

This poem enables children to:

▶ recognise the **ing** ending;

▶ say the **ing** ending;

▶ create a poem using the **ing** sound.

What you need

Things that go ding:

▶ empty tin cans

▶ triangles

▶ different size bells.

What you do

▶ Start by making the short 'i' sound. Open your mouth, smile and say a short sharp **i**.

▶ Now say ing. Repeat it until it sounds funny. Say **ing** once and ask the children to repeat it.

▶ Say **ing** any number of times and see if the children can repeat the same number of **ings** back.

See how many words you can think of that end in **ing**.

- ▶ Use pencils or beaters to gently hit a variety of objects, seeing if they make a ding sound.
- ▶ Read the poem and see if you can add new lines for the new objects you've found that go ding.

Further fun

You could:

Make your own bells

- ▶ Thread string through the top of empty tin cans. Check that there are no sharp edges. Cover the open end with tape to protect fingers. Hang them up and make them go ding!
- ▶ Go outside to see if you can find things that go ding.

Try gently hitting metal gates or railings with a pencil or beater.

EYFS Development matters statements

CLL (30-50m) Enjoy rhyming and rhyming activities.

CLL (30-50m) Show awareness of rhyme and alliteration.

PD (22-36m) Show increasing control in holding and using hammers, books, beaters and mark-making tools.

CD (22-36m) Create sounds by banging, shaking, tapping or blowing.

Hang up the washing

ang ang ang ang

Hang up the washing.
Hang up the washing.
Hang up the washing on the washing line.
Bang on the washing.
Bang on the washing.
Bang on the washing on the washing line.
Clang on the washing.
Clang on the washing.
Clang on the washing on the washing line.
Bang clang.
Bang clang.
Washing line.

This poem enables children to:

▶ recognise the **ang** ending;

▶ say the **ang** ending;

▶ create a poem using the 'ang' sound.

What you need

▶ string or similar for a washing line   ▶ scissors
▶ yoghurt pots   ▶ pencils or beaters

I will need

What you do

▶ Start by saying the short 'a' sound. Open your mouths wide and say the short 'a' sound as quickly and sharply as you can.

▶ Now say **ang**. Repeat it until it sounds funny. Say **ang** once and ask the children to repeat it.

- ▶ Say **ang** any number of times and see if they can repeat the same number of **angs** back

- ▶ See how many words you can think of that end with **ang**. Make a washing line by suspending a length of string from two points in your setting

- ▶ Cut shorter lengths of string and attach an empty yoghurt pot at each end by making a hole in the base, threading one end of the string through and knotting it. Do the same at the other end.

Read the rhyme and hang, bang and clang your pots as you say it.

Further fun

- ▶ Hang different things from your washing line; examples of writing or painting, or samples of craft work.

EYFS Development matters statements

CLL (30-50m) Show awareness of rhyme and alliteration.

PD (22-36m) Show increasing control in holding and using hammers, books, beaters and mark-making tools.

CD (22-36m) Create sounds by banging, shaking, tapping or blowing.

Hand Land

What happens in Hand Land?
Trees grow in Hand Land.
Fish swim in Hand Land.
Flowers bloom in Hand Land.
Animals play in Hand Land.
What else happens in Hand Land?

This poem enables children to:

▶ recognise the **and** ending;

▶ say the **and** ending;

▶ create a poem using the 'and' sound.

What you need—

▶ large sheets of paper

▶ finger paints

▶ materials for a collage: scraps of fabric, pictures from magazines etc.

▶ large felt pens

I will need

What you do

▶ Start by saying the short 'a' sound. Open your mouths wide and say the short 'a' sound as quickly and sharply as you can.

▶ Now say **and**, stressing the 'd' sound at the end. Say **and** once and ask the children to repeat it.

▶ Say **and** any number of times and see if they can repeat the same number of **ands** back.

▶ See how many words you can think of that end in **and**.

▶ Read the poem 'Hand Land', listening carefully for the words that have the **and** ending. Ask the children to put their hands up when they hear one.

Making Hand Land

▶ Divide a large piece of paper into four sections to create an area at the top for sky, in the middle for land, then a band of sea, and an area for sand at the bottom.

▶ Paint the top quarter with a light wash of pale blue, the next with a light wash of pale green, then a wash of blue again for the sea, and the bottom quarter a pale yellow for the sand.

▶ Make prints of the children's hands and cut them out.

▶ Now you can place the children's hand prints on your scene to create trees, birds, flowers, seaweed, shells, animals, fish etc.

Decorate the hand prints with collage materials to make eyes on your animals or fabric strips to make seaweed on the sand. Use thick felt pens to create detail.

Further fun

You could:

▶ Add more lines of your own to the poem. How many more **ands** can you add?

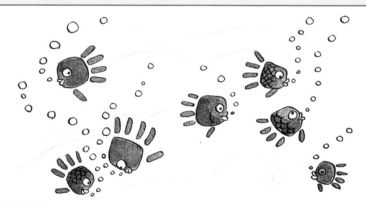

EYFS Development matters statements

CLL (30-50m) Enjoy rhyming and rhyming activities.

CLL (30-50m) Show awareness of rhyme and alliteration.

CLL (30-50m) Join in with repeated refrains and anticipate key events and phrases in rhymes and stories.

CD (30-50m) Capture experiences and responses with music, dance, paint and other materials or words.

What can I bend?

end end end end
end end end end

What can you send me to bend?
What can you send me to bend?
Can I bend a pencil?
Can I bend a block?
What can you send me to bend?

What can I send you to bend?
What can I send you to bend?
I can send you some dough.
I can send you some string.
That's what I'll send you to bend.

This poem enables children to:

▶ recognise the **end** ending;

▶ say the **end** ending;

▶ create a poem using the 'end' sound.

What you need

▶ your voices

▶ objects that will bend; dough, plasticine, rubber bands, pipe cleaners etc.

▶ objects that won't bend; pencils, wooden rulers, blocks etc.

What you do

▶ Start by saying the short 'e' sound. Open your mouths wide and say the short 'e' sound as quickly and sharply as you can.

▶ Now say **end**, stressing the 'd' sound at the end. Say **end** once and ask the children to repeat it.

▶ Say **end** any number of times and see if they can repeat the same number of **ends** back.

▶ See how many words you can think of that end with **end**, for example, end, bend, send, mend and pretend.

▶ Read the poem. Ask the children to say the word **bend** at the end of each line. Bend your fingers as you say the word.

▶ Look for things in your setting that will or won't bend. Add these to the poem.

▶ Look outside for things that will and won't bend. Add these to the poem.

Further fun

▶ Replace the word **bend** in the poem with the word **mend**: what things could you send to mend?

EYFS Development matters statements

CLL (30-50m) Enjoy rhyming and rhyming activities.

CLL (30-50m) Show awareness of rhyme and alliteration.

CLL (40-60+m) Continue a rhyming string.

PD (40-60+m) Explore malleable materials by patting, stroking, poking, squeezing, pinching and twisting them.

Section

Words are like blocks (build them!)

In this section, you will find four poems that deal with different types of words. These are words that do different jobs: words that are the names of things, words that describe things, words that are actions and words that describe the way we can do actions. These words do all have special names: nouns, verbs, adjectives and adverbs.

The labelling of nouns, verbs, adjectives and adverbs is an advanced skill for children in the Early Years, but it is not too early to introduce the idea that there are different types of words and that these words have different 'jobs'. Looking at poems and creating poetry together is an excellent way of understanding the 'jobs' words do and the way we can use these words to communicate our thoughts, feelings and ideas.

A noun is the name of an object, person or place:

cat, **chair**, **Jenny** and **London** are examples of nouns.

A verb is a word that describes an action:

jump, **run**, **hop** and **sleep** are examples of verbs.

An adjective is a word that describes something:

hot, **cold**, **red** and **soft** are examples of adjectives.

An adverb is a word that describes an action:

slowly, **quickly**, **quietly** and **loudly** are examples of adjectives.

I spy!

I spy with my clever eye things all around.
I spy with my clever eye things from sky to ground.
I spy a table. I spy! I spy!
I spy a chair. I spy! I spy!
I spy a block. I spy! I spy!
I spy a pencil. I spy! I spy!
I spy with my clever eye things all around.
I spy with my clever eye things from sky to ground.

Nouns are words that are the names of things, people or places.

This poem enables children to:

▶ understand that some words are the names of things
▶ explore the names of things
▶ improve memory skills
▶ create a poem using naming words.

What you need

▶ a tray
▶ seven familiar objects
▶ a cloth to cover the tray

What you do

▶ Talk about all the different types of toys you have in your setting.

▶ Can you see ten toys from where you are sitting?

▶ Can you make a list? Write a list with the children's help and display it.

▶ Talk about the fact we all have names and that things have names too, such as 'table', 'chair', 'pencil' and 'plant'.

▶ Read the poem, then try to remember all the objects mentioned in the poem. How many can the children remember? Can anybody remember all of them without any help?

▶ Read the poem again and see how many you can remember this time.

▶ Make up new lines for the poem using objects you can see in your setting.

Further fun

▶ Play the memory game with objects found on a nature walk.

▶ Write the poem using objects found on a nature walk.

Play the memory game

▶ Place seven familiar objects on a tray. Allow the children to look at them for a few minutes, then cover the tray and see how many objects they can remember.

EYFS Development matters statements

PSED (40-60+m) Maintain attention, concentrate and sit quietly when appropriate.

CLL (30-50m) Understand the concept of a word.

CLL (40-60+m) Extend their vocabulary, exploring the meanings and sounds of new words.

CLL (40-60+m) Extend vocabulary, especially by grouping or naming things.

KUW (30-50m) Show curiosity and interest in the features of objects and living things.

What can I do?

Do, do, what can I do?
I can do so much.
Do, do what can I do?
Why don't you come and watch?
Watch me, watch me, watch me...
Jump!
Jump! Jump! Jump!
Watch me, watch me, watch me...
Run!
Run! Run! Run!
Watch me, watch me, watch me...
Wiggle!
Wiggle! Wiggle! Wiggle!
Do, do, what can I do?
I can do so much!

Verbs are words that are actions.

What you need

▶ your voices
▶ your bodies

This poem enables children to:

▶ understand that some words describe actions;
▶ explore words that describe actions;
▶ create a poem using action words.

What you do

▶ Read the poem and join in with the actions.
▶ See if you can think of other actions. Prompt the children by doing the actions yourself and asking them to guess what you are doing.
▶ Can they hop, skip, spin or roll?

Recreate the poem together, adding your own favourite actions.

Further fun

You could play:

Simon Says

▶ Say 'Simon says', followed by an action. The children should then copy that action.

▶ Say an action without saying 'Simon says' first. Anyone who does the action is out.

Actions could include:

▶ rub your tummy

▶ scratch your nose

▶ run on the spot

▶ jump up and down.

Play 'Simon Says' outside with bigger actions, such as 'Simon says run to the fence' or 'Simon says take five big jumps forward'.

EYFS Development matters statements

CLL (30-50m) Build up a vocabulary that reflects the breadth of their experience.

CLL (40-60+m) Extend their vocabulary, exploring the meanings and sounds of new words.

PD (22-36m) Manage body to create intended movements.

PD (40-60+m) Move with control and coordination.

What am I?

I am blue.
I am pointy.
I am long.
I am shiny
I am thin.
What am I?
I am a pencil!

This poem enables children to:

▶ become familiar with descriptive language;

▶ recognise words that have the job of describing things;

▶ create a poem that uses describing words.

Adjectives are words that describe things.

What you need

▶ your voices

▶ a large box or bag

▶ a variety of objects

▶ shredded newspaper

What you do

▶ Choose some objects from your setting. Place them in a large box or bag with some shredded newspaper.

▶ Take it in turns to pick out an object.

▶ Examine the object and answer these questions:

  ▶ What colour is it?

  ▶ Is it hard or soft?

  ▶ Is it shiny?

  ▶ Is it big or small?

  ▶ Is it rough or smooth?

  ▶ What is it?

▶ Choose an item as a subject to create your own poem together using 'What am I?' as a model.

Further fun

  ▶ Go on a nature walk and find some interesting objects to describe.

  ▶ Go on an urban walk and describe an interesting building.

EYFS Development matters statements

PSRN (22-36m) Begin to categorise objects according to properties such as shape or size.

CLL (40-60+m) Extend their vocabulary, exploring the meanings and sounds of new words.

KUW (30-50m) Show curiosity and interest in the features of objects and living things.

KUW (30-50m) Describe and talk about what they see.

Quickly, slowly

Slowly, slowly, what goes slowly?
What can creep and crawl?
Slowly, slowly, what goes slowly?
All things big and small.
A slug, a snail, a tortoise too.
A worm, a beetle, me and you.
Quickly, quickly, what goes quickly?
What can zip and whiz?
Quickly, quickly, what goes quickly?
All things small and big.
A train, a car, a motorbike too.
A tiger, a lion, me and you.
Quickly, quickly, what goes quickly?
What can zip and whiz?
Slowly, slowly, what goes slowly?
All things big and small.

Adverbs are words that describe actions.

This poem enables children to:
► describe actions
► recognise a word that describes an action
► create a poem that uses action descriptions.

What you need
► your voices
► your bodies

What you do
► Discuss different things you could do quickly or slowly. Can they walk slowly? Eat slowly? Talk slowly? Can they do these things quickly?

Play 'Quick, quick, slow'.

▶ Sit the children in the largest space you have available.

▶ Ask them to run, jump, skip or hop either quickly or slowly. Change actions and repeat. Read the poem and see if you can add more things that move either quickly or slowly.

Further fun

▶ If you have limited space or wish to keep the children seated, you could play 'Quick, quick, slow' with hand and arm actions only. Can they wiggle their fingers slowly? Can they pat their tummy quickly? Can they touch their nose slowly? Can they flap their elbows quickly?

▶ Make a quick and slow display. Collect pictures of things that move quickly and slowly. Place the things that move quickly on one side of the display and the things that move slowly on the other.

EYFS Development matters statements

CLL (30-50m) Begin to use more complex sentences.

CLL (40-60+m) Extend their vocabulary, exploring the meanings and sounds of new words.

PD (22-36m) Manage body to create intended movements.

Section

Putting it together

This section gives a selection of poems that can be used as templates for your own poetry creation. These activities are suitable for Reception children who have the necessary literacy skills to begin to create written work themselves. Younger children can change the words with the practitioner, scribing and recording their creations if appropriate. The activities invite you to change the poems to make them your own. The poems are frameworks – you can add or take away words or phrases according to your needs.

My best toy

My best toy is yellow and pink.
My best toy is soft.
My best toy is small.

My best toy is my doll.
I love my best toy.

This poem enables children to:

▶ create their own poem about a favourite toy.

What you need

▶ each child's favourite toy
▶ the poem 'My best toy'

What you do

▶ Ask the children to think of their favourite toy.
▶ Ask the following questions:
  ▶ What colour or colours is it?
  ▶ Is it hard or soft?
  ▶ Is it big or small?

- ▶ Using the poem 'My best toy' as a model, create your own poems by making lines about each child's best toy.
- ▶ Write these or print them for the children.
- ▶ Can they learn to recite them?

Further fun

- ▶ Display your poems with the toys you've described or take photographs of the toys and display them alongside the poems.

EYFS Development matters statements

CLL (30-50m) Use a widening range of words to express or elaborate on ideas.

PSRN (22-36m) Begin to categorise objects according to properties such as shape or size.

KUW (30-50m) Show curiosity and interest in the features of objects and living things.

KUW (30-50m) Describe and talk about what they see.

The person in the mirror

The person in the mirror has long hair.
The person in the mirror has brown hair.
The person in the mirror has brown eyes.
The person in the mirror
is wearing a yellow jumper.
The person in the mirror is me!

This poem enables children to:

▶ describe themselves

▶ create a poem about themselves.

What you need

▶ mirrors

What you do

▶ Read the poem The person in the mirror, focusing on the descriptive language.

▶ Discuss different hair colours and styles.

▶ Discuss eye colour.

▶ Using the person in the mirror as the subject, create your own poems.

Further fun

▶ Use dressing-up props to pretend to be different people. Describe them in a poem.

EYFS Development matters statements

PSED (40-60+m) Have a positive self-image and show that they are comfortable with themselves.

KUW (30-50m) Show curiosity and interest in the features of objects and living things.

KUW (30-50m) Describe and talk about what they see.

Food fun

I like soup, I can slurp it.
I like toffee, I can chew it.
I like apples, I can munch them.
I like carrots, I can crunch them.

Slurp, munch, crunch, chew.
Food gives me lots of things to do.

This poem enables children to:

▶ discuss different foods

▶ discuss food preference

▶ discuss words that describe eating food

▶ create a poem about food.

What you need

▶ play food
▶ pictures of different foods from magazines

What you do

▶ Look at different types of food and discuss what each one would be like to eat.

▶ Would it be hot or cold? Plain or spicy? Crunchy or soft?

▶ Using the poem as a template, create lines of your own.

Further fun

▶ Play restaurants. Make menus with pictures of food taken from magazines.
▶ Pretend to have a meal. Are you crunching and munching, slurping and chewing?

EYFS Development matters statements

PSED (30-50m) Make connections between different parts of their life experience.

CLL (40-60+m) Extend their vocabulary, exploring the meanings and sounds of new words.

Outside explorers

We are the outside explorers,
We are the find out more-ers,
We are the out-of-the-door-ers.
What can we find?

We find tall trees.
We find green grass.
We find crunchy leaves.
We find smooth stones.
We find long streets.
We find big shops.

We are the outside explorers,
We are the find out more-ers,
We are the out-of-the-door-ers.

See what we've found!

This poem enables children to:

▶ explore descriptive language;

▶ talk about the outdoor environment;

▶ record their findings.

What you need

▶ recording equipment such as notebooks, cameras, scrapbooks and collecting bags

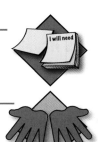

What you do

▶ Be outdoor explorers. Go for a walk outside your setting. This can be a nature walk or a walk around the local environment.

▶ Encourage the children to write or draw pictures in their explorer notebooks or take pictures with a camera. Discuss the things you see.

▶ Using the poem as a template, add your own findings to create your own poem.

Further fun

▶ Use magnifying glasses to observe things closely.

▶ What does a brick look like under a magnifying glass? What does a blade of grass look like? Think of interesting words to describe your findings.

EYFS Development matters statements

CLL (30-50m) Use writing as a means of recording and communicating.

CLL (40-60+m) Extend their vocabulary, exploring the meanings and sounds of new words.

PSRN (22-36m) Begin to categorise objects according to properties such as shape or size.

KUW (40-60+m) Notice differences between features of the local environment.

KUW (30-50m) Describe and talk about what they see.

Animals aloud!

A cat says miaow and licks its fur.
A dog says woof and wags its tail.

The mouse says squeak and runs away.
But I say hello and can play all day.

A bird says tweet and makes a nest.
A duck says quack and swims on a pond.

The mouse says squeak and runs away.
But I say hello and can play all day.

This poem enables children to:

▶ talk about animal features

▶ understand the difference between various animals and people

▶ create a poem about animals.

What you need

▶ toy animals or pictures of animals

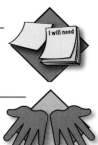

What you do

▶ Look at each of your toy animals in turn and ask what noise their animal equivalents make.

▶ Make the animal noise together.

▶ Ask where the animal lives or what it does.

▶ Pretend to be animals. Put the toy animals or pictures in a bag and ask the children to pick one out and pretend to be that animal. Can they move like that animal? Can they make the sound of that animal? Does it have a tail to swish? After a few minutes, pick another animal and repeat.

▶ Using the poem as a template, create your own lines for the poem.

Further fun

▶ Make animal masks to display with your poem by painting and decorating paper plates to look like animal faces.

EYFS Development matters statements ————————

CLL (40-60+m) Explore and experiment with sounds, words and texts.

CLL (40-60+m) Listen with enjoyment and respond to stories and songs, and make up their own stories and poems.

Colour poems

Red, yellow, pink and green.
So many colours to be seen.
Colours dark and colours bright
How many red things can we find?

Roses.
Strawberries.
Ribbons.
And beads.

These are the red things we can find.

This poem enables children to:

▶ describe objects using colours

▶ become familiar with a wide range of colours

▶ use colour in a poem.

What you need

▶ samples of objects in different colours – these can be anything that you have available

What you do

▶ Read through the poem.

▶ See how many red things you can find in your setting and make a list of them.

▶ Using the poem as a template, choose a different colour for line four and then list things that are that colour. Write the poem together and display your work.

▶ Explore more colour words, such as purple, orange and grey.

Further fun

▶ Make a cloud colour poem. Start with the sentence 'Clouds are white'. Then create a list of different things that are white to make different descriptions of white.

Use these items to describe a kind of white.
For example:

Clouds are white
Clouds are snow white.
Clouds are pillowcase white.
Clouds are tissue white.
Clouds are milk white.

You can use the same method for the sentence 'The sky is blue' or 'The trees are green'. Use your imagination and think of some more!

EYFS Development Statements

CLL (22-36m) Show interest and play with sounds and rhymes.

CLL (30-50m) Enjoy rhyming and rhyming activities.

CD (30-50m) Explore colour and begin to differentiate between colours.

Poetry websites

www.literacytrust.org.uk/Database/poetry.html

Website for the Literacy trust. Contains up-to-date information on literacy matters.

www.barbican.org.uk/canihaveaword/

Contains resources for creative writing and features work by leading children's poets.

www.maninthemoon.co.uk/

A useful resource for poetry written by children.

www.nawe.co.uk

Website for the National Association of Writers in Education. Contains a list of writers available to work in schools.

www.poetryclass.net/index.htm

Poetry Society website. Contains many useful resources and links to children's poetry sites.